THE ULTIMATE GUIDE TO DIVORCE CASES IN TEXAS

Busting Myths and Avoiding the 10 Deadly Sins That Can Wreck Your Case

BRYAN JOSEPH FAGAN, ESQ.

For more information or permissions, contact:

Bryan Joseph Fagan

Law Office of Bryan Fagan PLLC
3707 Cypress Creek Pkwy,
Houston, TX 77068
Tel: (281) 810-9760
Fax: (855) 668-0536
www.bryanfagan.com

FIRST EDITION
ISBN-13: 978-1-7328903-2-9

LEGAL DISCLAIMER

This book is not intended to provide legal advice. It offers general information about Texas divorce law for educational purposes only.

Every divorce is different. Laws change. Situational outcomes depend on specific facts, timing, and strategy. You should consult a licensed attorney before making any legal decisions. Nothing in this publication constitutes an attorney–client relationship.

There is no substitute for in-person advice from a qualified, experienced attorney who understands your specific situation.

Table of Contents

FOREWORD:

Why This Book and Why Now?

Divorce is one of the most consequential legal events most people will ever face. And yet, most enter the process unprepared, overwhelmed, and unsure who to trust.

After years of representing families across Texas, I noticed one pattern that became impossible to ignore. People do not usually make bad decisions in a divorce because they do not care. They make them because they lack clear information when they need it most. I wrote this book to try to change that.

At the Law Office of Bryan Fagan, PLLC, we have seen firsthand how confusion, pressure, and misinformation derail otherwise reasonable cases. We have also seen how clarity, when paired with strategy, can dramatically improve outcomes.

A Method Built from Experience

Over time, we have identified recurring mistakes that consistently cause damage to our clients. These are not legal technicalities, but behavioral and strategic errors—the **Deadly Sins of Divorce**—that turn manageable cases into costly ones.

This book breaks those mistakes down and shows you how to avoid them. This guidance is not theoretical. It reflects real cases and outcomes, as well as the same framework we use every day to help clients protect their children, finances, and future.

Information Changes Outcomes

Knowing how divorce operates helps people make smarter choices. They communicate more effectively. They preserve credibility with the court. They avoid regret.

Whether you are considering divorce, are already in the process, or are trying to regain control of a case that's gone off the rails, this book is meant to give you a fresh perspective before pressure forces you to make rash decisions.

Read this book carefully. Mark it up. Return to it when your emotions run high. And, if you decide you want personalized guidance, my team and I are here to help. What matters most is that you do not move forward unthinkingly.

Wishing you clarity, strength, peace, and steadiness as you take your next steps,

Bryan Fagan, Esq.
Attorney & Founder
The Law Office of Bryan Fagan, PLLC

CHAPTER 1:

Taking Control and Navigating Family Law with Confidence and Clarity

Most people do not realize until they are living it that divorce is not just a legal process. It is an emotional one, a financial one, a parenting one. It is deeply human.

If you are reading this, you may feel overwhelmed, afraid, or stuck. You may not know your rights, your next steps, or even what questions to ask. That's normal. Almost everyone I meet at the beginning of a divorce feels that way. But what I want you to know from the start is that you do not have to do this alone, and you do not have to figure everything out today. You have to take the first step deliberately, not emotionally.

Divorce Feels Chaotic Because It is Unfamiliar

Divorce throws people off-balance because it is unfamiliar territory. Most of us are never taught how family law works. We rely on stories from friends, advice from relatives, or things we have seen online or on television. Much of that information is wrong.

When people do not understand the process, fear of the unknown leads to rushed decisions, unnecessary conflict, and mistakes that can affect children, finances, and long-term stability. This book aims to close that gap.

Why I Believe Clarity Changes Outcomes

When I founded my firm in 2012, I didn't set out to build the largest family law practice in Texas. I wanted to create a place where people could find clarity amid chaos and be treated with honesty, empathy, and practical guidance.

Over the years, I've seen the same patterns. People who understand what is happening in their cases make better decisions. They communicate more effectively. They protect their credibility. They experience less regret. That doesn't mean divorce is easy, but it can be manageable.

What Taking Control Really Means

Taking control does not mean being aggressive or "winning at all costs". It does not mean knowing every detail of the law. Taking control means:

- Understanding what matters and what doesn't
- Making decisions based on facts
- Knowing when to act and when to pause
- Asking for help before mistakes can compound

In this book, I will walk you through how divorce actually works in Texas, without legal jargon, worst-case scenarios, or scare tactics. My goal is to help you feel grounded enough to make decisions you won't regret later.

What Happens When You Reach Out

When people contact my office, they are often nervous. They expect judgment or a sales pitch. That's not how we operate.

What they get is a conversation with someone who listens first, then clearly explains their options. They speak with someone who helps them understand what comes next without rushing them to make any decisions. Whether a case is simple or complex, cooperative or filled with conflict, the goal is the same: clarity, strategy, and steady guidance.

My Promise Moving Forward

I believe family law should empower people, not intimidate them. You should understand what is happening in your case and why certain decisions are being made. You should never feel ignored or as if you must hurry through one of the most important periods of your life.

This book is meant to give you perspective rather than pressure, information instead of fear, and direction over noise. You do not need to be "ready". You need to be informed. Once you take that first step with clarity, everything that follows becomes that much easier to navigate.

📞 Call us today at (281) 810-9760
🌐 or visit www.bryanfagan.com

The first step is often the hardest, but it is also the most important one. Let's take it together.

"We meet people during some of the hardest moments of their lives, and we get to help them. That's not just our job. That's our purpose."

~ Bryan Joseph Fagan, Esq.

CHAPTER 2:

Why I Built the Law Office of Bryan Fagan

When you are going through a divorce or custody case, everything feels personal. That's because it is. You are not just dealing with paperwork or court dates, but with your children, your finances, your home, and your future.

That's why choosing the right law firm matters. Not every firm is built to handle that level of pressure with clarity, professionalism, and care. Not every firm is designed to support people who feel overwhelmed, scared, or unsure of what comes next. I built the Law Office of Bryan Fagan to be different—not just in how we practice law, but in how we treat people overall.

Resilience, Growth, and a Mission to Serve Texan Families

When I opened the doors in 2012, I was not trying to build one of the largest family law firms in Texas. My goal was to support others, especially families similar to mine. That vision hasn't changed. What changed was the demand.

As more people came to us for help, the firm grew. Our team now includes over 170 legal professionals, including attorneys and paralegals, who primarily handle family law cases throughout Harris County and nearby areas. We take on select cases throughout the rest of Texas. But size alone doesn't define a firm. What matters most is how it performs in difficult circumstances.

A Firm Shaped by Real-World Challenges

Over the years, the firm has been tested in ways no business plan can predict. In 2017, Hurricane Harvey flooded our office. Because we had already adopted cloud-based organizational systems, client data remained secure, and we were operational again within a week. We worked on cardboard tables and our cell phones, with no small amount of determination. In 2020, when COVID-19 shut down courtrooms across Texas, we adopted remote operations almost overnight to keep cases moving along as smoothly as possible. In 2021, a historic winter storm crippled infrastructure statewide, but our systems stayed live, and our clients got the support they needed. In 2024, when Hurricane Beryl caused widespread outages, we operated with a skeleton crew to ensure no active case was left unattended. Every challenge reinforced the importance of preparation, adaptability, and commitment, reminding us that these matter just as much as any legal knowledge.

What We Do and Why It Matters

Our practice focuses on legal issues that hit closest to home, including divorce, custody and visitation, child support, adoption, CPS defense, marital agreements, and select estate planning matters. However, our work also goes beyond legal filings and court appearances. We help people:

- Protect their relationships with their children
- Rebuild financial stability
- Make informed, confident decisions
- Navigate uncertainty with a clear plan

We do not take those responsibilities lightly.

The Principles That Guide Our Work

Over time, I've identified a few core principles that consistently help lead to better outcomes for clients. They shape how we handle every case.

We educate before we litigate. Confusion creates fear, but education creates confidence. Clients deserve to understand their rights, the risks, and their options in plain English, not legal jargon or worst-case scenarios.

We put clients in control. Whether someone works with our legal team in person or uses our Online Divorce Service, transparency matters. Clients should always know where their case stands and what is coming next.

We respect time as well as money. Divorce is expensive enough without surprises. Clear communication and responsible billing are essential practices, not optional.

We embrace progress. Family law doesn't have to feel outdated. Secure messaging, virtual court appearances, and flexible technology help clients stay connected and informed wherever they are.

We hire competent, compassionate professionals. Legal skill matters, but so does empathy. Every member of our team is trained to handle emotionally charged situations professionally and respectfully.

We Know What People Are Really Facing

Some people who come to us are afraid they will lose custody of their children. Some come after their spouse has already moved out. Others need someone to explain what is happening and help them slow down. No two situations are identical, but the emotions are often the same: uncertainty, fear of making the wrong decision, and feeling pressured to act before understanding the consequences. That's when good legal guidance matters the most.

It is Not About Winning, but About Doing What is Right

Clients sometimes ask about win-loss records, but family law doesn't have a scoreboard. What matters is what is fair and strategic, as well as what protects your future, especially when children are involved. Our approach focuses on long-term stability, not short-term emotional victories. This philosophy has guided the firm since day one. This is why the firm grew, and why people trust us during some of the most difficult moments of their lives.

Ready When You Are

Picking up the phone and calling a divorce lawyer can feel intimidating. Most people do not call because they feel ready, but because they feel overwhelmed. What I've learned over the years is simply that people who reach out early on tend to make better decisions and experience fewer regrets. That being said, the goal is not to rush, but to be informed. When you do that, you put yourself back in control—where you belong.

CHAPTER 3:

Myths You Might Have Heard from Friends, Neighbors, or Relatives

Divorce is a life-altering journey. It comes with legal twists, emotional turns, and, unfortunately, a steady stream of misinformation.

You are not alone if you have ever been cornered at a family gathering, in a group chat, or over coffee by someone offering confident "divorce advice". Most people going through a divorce hear more opinions than facts, and those opinions often come from well-meaning friends, opinionated relatives, or people who repeat stories they only understand at a very basic level.

The problem is not that people want to help. The problem is that divorce myths spread quickly and leave a lot of damage in their wake. Whether you are just beginning to think about getting a divorce, already in the middle of one, or simply trying to understand your options, this chapter is designed to help you separate fact from fiction and move forward with clarity, not confusion.

Why Divorce Myths Persist

Most divorce myths seem to come from the same places.

- Outdated legal information
- One person's experience is a universal rule
- Television dramas or horror stories circulated via social media
- Emotional biases and misunderstanding of Texas law

For example, someone might insist that their friend "lost the house" simply because they moved out during a separation period. They usually leave out the rest of the story: a court order, financial misconduct, or a strategic mistake that had nothing to do with their moving out. Divorce is complex, and when emotions run high, incomplete information spreads quickly.

Why This Matters

Believing the wrong information can be costly. I've seen people give up rights they didn't need to surrender, make rash decisions they later regretted, and fail to protect what mattered most because they relied on myths instead of facts. When it comes to divorce, knowledge is not just power; it is protection. This chapter is about replacing fear-based advice with clarity. In the chapters that follow, I will walk you through some of the most common divorce myths I've heard.

- "The mother always wins custody of the children."
- "If you move out of the house, you lose it in the divorce."
- "You can avoid paying child support by quitting your job."

- "If your spouse cheated, they lose everything."
- "You do not need a lawyer. Just use online forms."

Each myth will be broken down so you understand:

- Where it comes from
- Why does it get repeated
- What Texas law actually dictates
- What you should do instead of acting on these myths

You'll also read up on real-world examples and practical guidance designed to help you avoid common—and often expensive—mistakes.

Busting Myths Is How You Take Control

I often tell clients that one of the most powerful things they can do during a divorce is to stop guessing.

Imagine someone confidently announcing at a party, "If your spouse cheats, they lose everything in the divorce."

Once you have read this book, you'll understand what the law allows, how courts really process cases, and how to respond strategically instead of emotionally. You won't just know what the myths are; you'll know how to see through them.

A Few Important Reminders

Before we dive in, keep three things in mind:

1. **Every divorce is different.** Your finances, parenting history, and goals are more important than others' experiences.
2. **Texas law is unique.** This book focuses on the Texas Family Code and the Texas courts. While some principles apply elsewhere, these details matter.
3. **This book is educational, not personal legal advice.** Use it to be informed, then consult with a qualified family law attorney about your specific situation.

CHAPTER 4:

Myth #1:
The Mother Always Wins Custody of the Children

I hear this myth more than almost any other. Someone leans in at a family gathering, lowers their voice, and says, "You know, the mother always wins custody of the children."

That belief is one of the most persistent myths in family law and one of the most damaging. It is not just outdated; it also discourages good parents, especially fathers, from asserting their rights and staying fully involved in their children's lives. Let's set the record straight.

Where This Myth Came From

At one point in history, this myth had some truth to it. Courts across the country once followed what was known as the tender years' doctrine. Under that approach, children were presumed to be better off with their mothers, particularly during early childhood years. Fathers were often limited to visitation only, regardless of their involvement or capabilities.

However, family structures evolved. The responsibilities of parents have evolved. The law changed with them. Today, Texas courts follow a very different standard.

The Only Standard That Matters in Texas

Every custody decision in Texas is guided by one principle: **what is in the best interest of the child** (Texas Family Code §153.002).

That's it. Judges are not allowed to favor one parent based on gender. They are required to evaluate facts, behavior, and the child's long-term well-being.

What Courts Actually Look at Today

In Texas, judges decide conservatorship based on several factors, without favoring either parent.

Stability and safety: Which parent can provide a safe, stable, and consistent home environment?

Parental involvement: who takes the child to school, attends medical appointments, helps with homework, and participates in daily life?

Willingness to co-parent: Courts value cooperation. A parent who supports the child's relationship with the other parent is often viewed more favorably than one who undermines it.

History of caretaking: judges consider who has handled day-to-day responsibilities in the past, without assuming those roles were based on gender.

Each parent's overall capabilities: mental health, work schedules, home conditions, and emotional availability all matter. Gender does not.

Fathers in Texas Family Court Today

Modern Texas courts recognize that fathers are just as capable as mothers of raising children. In many cases, judges award **joint managing conservatorship**, meaning both parents share legal rights and responsibilities, even if possession schedules differ. The stereotype that fathers do not win meaningful custody doesn't hold up in today's courts.

The Real Takeaway

Custody decisions are not about "mother knows best," but about what is best for the child. Judges aren't handing out trophies based on biology. They are looking at evidence, a person's conduct, and their long-term stability. If you are an involved, responsible, and cooperative parent, you have a real chance of maintaining a meaningful role in your child's life, regardless of your gender.

How to Handle This Myth

The next time someone tells you that the mom always gets the kids, you can calmly respond:

- Texas courts do not favor one parent over the other.
- Custody decisions are based on facts, not stereotypes.
- Fathers succeed in custody cases all the time when they stay involved and focused on their children.

If that person is still not convinced, you can always suggest they speak with a Texas family law attorney who handles these cases every day.

CHAPTER 5:

Myth #2:
Divorce Always Means a Long Battle in Court

Popular television has done divorce no favors. If your understanding of divorce comes from TV dramas, you'd probably expect to encounter furious spouses, courtroom theatrics, and a judge slamming a gavel while issuing life-changing decisions, and all in a single afternoon. It makes for compelling television, but it does not reflect how most divorces in Texas actually unfold.

The Short Answer

Most divorces in Texas are resolved outside the courtroom. While litigation is sometimes necessary, most families choose paths that avoid the emotional toll, financial strain, and extended timelines of full trials. In many cases, the court is a safety net, not the main event.

How Most Texas Divorces Are Really Resolved

There are several established alternatives to a courtroom battle, and they account for the resolution of most cases.

Mediation is one of the most common and effective ways to resolve a divorce. A neutral third party, usually a retired judge or family law expert, facilitates communication and negotiation to reach an agreement. Mediation works because it is private, efficient, and cost-effective. It allows people to speak openly without the fear that every word will later be used against them. In many Texas counties, mediation is required before a case can even proceed to trial. For couples who can still communicate, even if imperfectly, mediation is often the fastest path to resolution.

Collaborative law is a structured, team-based approach where both parties and their attorneys commit to resolving the case without litigation. Financial professionals and parenting specialists may also get involved to help craft thoughtful solutions that benefit the entire family. This approach works best in cases involving complex finances or heightened emotions, and both sides still want to avoid trial. Everyone signs an agreement committing to settlement, which keeps the process focused on the future rather than adversarial tactics for the present.

Attorney-led negotiation applies in many divorces. Attorneys negotiate directly with one another behind the scenes to help ensure that legal rights are protected without forcing clients into court appearances or public conflict. The court is considered a last resort rather than a strategy. Many clients are surprised to learn that a divorce can be resolved without them ever having to step into a courtroom.

Even when a divorce is contested, many issues can be resolved through **pretrial conferences**. These meetings allow a judge to clarify issues, encourage settlement, and narrow down what truly needs to be decided. Judges generally prefer resolution, especially in cases involving children, and often actively work to avoid unnecessary trials.

Why Avoiding Trial Is Often the Smartest Move

Resolving a divorce outside of trial offers real advantages. For one, trials are expensive; legal fees can accumulate quickly when a case is fully litigated. They are also emotionally draining; a public courtroom battle can worsen conflict and leave lasting scars. Trials can take months or even years to resolve, and they remove control from both parties. A judge makes the final decisions, not the family.

When cases settle, people retain more control over their finances, their parenting plans, and their future.

The Real Takeaway

Divorce does not have to be a war. It can be a deliberate process that protects your children, your finances, and your long-term stability. While some cases do require court intervention, most do not resemble the dramatic showdowns people have come to expect. The idea that divorce always equals years of courtroom conflict is a myth that makes people afraid when they do not need to be.

CHAPTER 6:

Myth #3:
Assets Are Always Divided Equally

I often hear people assume that divorce works like simple arithmetic.

"Everything gets split in half, right?"

That idea sounds reasonable, but it is usually wrong. Dividing assets in a Texas divorce is far more complex. If you have been lying awake at night imagining your retirement account automatically being cut in half for the sake of your divorce, it is time to clear up the confusion.

The Short Answer

No, assets are not always divided equally in a Texas divorce. Why? Because divorce is not math. It is the law. Texas law focuses on what is fair, not what is strictly equal. That distinction matters.

Community Property Does Not Mean Equal Property

Texas is a community property state, meaning that, in general, property acquired during the marriage belongs to both spouses. But, under Texas Family Code §7.001, courts must divide community property in a manner that is **"just and right, having due regard for the rights of each party."**

In plain terms, the court's job is to reach a fair outcome. While judges may begin with the idea of equal division, the final result depends entirely on the facts of the case.

What Courts Actually Consider

When deciding how to divide community property, Texas judges consider many factors, including:

Income and earning capacity: Does one spouse earn significantly more than the other? Did one spouse give up career opportunities to support the household or care for the children?

Contributions to the marriage: these are not limited to income. Raising children, managing the home, or supporting a spouse while they further their education all carry real weight.

Length of the marriage: Longer marriages may result in a more balanced division, while shorter marriages may lead courts to return spouses closer to their premarriage financial circumstances.

Future needs: ongoing medical expenses, disability, or child-related financial responsibilities can affect how property is divided.

Marital misconduct: if one spouse wasted community assets or otherwise harmed the marital estate, the court may adjust the division of property in light of that conduct.

A Practical Example

Imagine that you and your spouse built a valuable collection not because it was expensive, but because it mattered to one of you. A strict fifty-fifty split would divide the collection perfectly in half. A fair division might award the entire collection to the spouse who values it and give the other spouse property of equivalent value. That's how Texas courts approach property division: by looking at practical fairness rather than symmetry.

The Real Takeaway

The idea that everything is divided equally in a divorce is one of the more common misconceptions I encounter. In Texas, the goal is **practical fairness**. Courts look at the realities of the marriage, the needs of each spouse, and the long-term consequences of their decisions.

Property division can feel overwhelming, but when handled correctly, it often results in outcomes that reflect the real dynamics of the marriage, not just the balance sheet.

CHAPTER 7:

Myth #4: I will Get a More Favorable Settlement If My Spouse Cheats

This myth sounds dramatic for a reason.

"If my spouse cheats, they lose everything in the divorce."

It feels emotionally satisfying. It also happens to be misleading, because while infidelity may hurt feelings, it doesn't automatically win you more in a divorce. Adultery can matter in a Texas divorce, but it does not guarantee that one spouse will walk away with everything while the other is punished. The real impact of infidelity depends on how it affects legally relevant issues.

The Short Answer

Yes, adultery can influence certain aspects of a divorce in Texas. No, it does not automatically result in a better settlement, more property, or sole custody for the other spouse. Texas courts are not designed to punish simply bad behavior, but to reach outcomes that are fair, lawful, and focused on long-term stability.

How Adultery Fits Into Texas Divorce Law

Texas is a fault-based divorce state, which means adultery can be pleaded as a ground for divorce under Texas Family Code §6.003. When properly proven, fault may be considered, particularly in property division.

Proof of adultery does not guarantee financial gain. Judges are not moral referees. They divide property in a just manner that is designed to protect the best interests of children.

When Infidelity Can Have Financial Consequences

Adultery becomes legally significant when it impacts the marital estate. For example, if a spouse spent community funds on affair vacations, gifts, hotel stays, housing, etc., a court may treat those expenditures as **marital waste**. In those cases, a judge may award the other spouse a larger share of the remaining community assets as compensation. If no community funds were misused, adultery alone is unlikely to affect the division of property in any meaningful way.

Custody Is About the Child, Not the Affair

Custody decisions in Texas are based on the best interests of the child, not whether one parent or the other was faithful. However, if an affair exposed a child to unsafe, unstable, or inappropriate circumstances—such as introducing a new partner prematurely or creating chaotic living conditions—that may be relevant. The focus is not the affair itself, but how a parent's conduct affects the child's safety and well-being.

A Practical Example

Imagine discovering that your spouse spent $12,000 of community funds on a luxury trip with someone with whom they were having an affair. That money may be classified as marital waste, and the court could adjust the property division to account for the loss. By contrast, if no community money was spent, the court may acknowledge the infidelity without imposing a financial penalty. The difference lies in the evidence, not the emotion it evokes.

Why Legal Guidance Matters

Adultery cases carry both legal and emotional weight. Without proper guidance, people often focus on proving the infidelity itself took place rather than what actually matters. An experienced divorce attorney can help determine:

- Whether marital waste is probable and financially significant
- How fault may realistically affect property division
- When pursuing adultery claims helps versus when it only increases conflict

The goal is not to get revenge. The goal is to fine-tune your legal strategy.

The Real Takeaway

Infidelity can matter in a Texas divorce, but it is rarely the dramatic turning point people expect it to be. Courts do not exist to punish adultery, but to divide property fairly, protect children, and resolve disputes according to the law. So, if someone tells you that if your spouse cheats, you get everything, you can safely take that advice with a grain of salt. Going through a divorce requires fairness and a sound strategy for all involved to move forward.

CHAPTER 8:

Myth #5: You Can Deny Your Spouse Visitation Rights If They Do not Pay Child Support

When emotions run high and bills pile up, resentment comes easily. This is especially true when a parent fails to pay court-ordered child support.

I often hear people say, "If they are not paying, why should they get to see the kids?"

That reaction is understandable, but it is also misguided from a legal standpoint.

The Short Answer

No, you cannot legally withhold visitation rights because child support hasn't been paid. In Texas, child support and visitation (or, possession and access) are two separate legal issues. One does not cancel the other. Parenting time is not a payment plan, and the law does not allow one parent to enforce support by interfering with the other's right to visitation. In fact, trying to do so often backfires.

Why Texas Law Keeps These Issues Separate

Child support and visitation both exist to protect the child, not to reward or punish parents.

Child support exists to provide for a child's financial needs, including food, housing, education, and health care. When support is not paid, the court can penalize the parent using tools such as wage garnishment, license suspension, tax refund interception, and contempt proceedings.

Visitation exists to preserve the child's relationships with both parents. Interfering with court-ordered visitation is itself a violation that can result in serious consequences.

Just because one parent fails to pay child support does not mean they lose their parental rights. Being the primary caregiver does not give one parent the authority to change a court-ordered schedule.

The Risks of Withholding Visitation

Withholding visitation can cause damage far beyond the immediate dispute, especially to the child.

It can harm the child. Courts view the parent-child relationship as fundamental. Denying access may be seen as parental alienation, which can emotionally harm the child and raise serious concerns in court.

It can harm your case. Parents who do this risk being held in contempt, fined, or, in severe cases, having custody or visitation modified in favor of the other parent. Even when a parent is not paying support, judges expect the other to continue to follow the law.

What to Do Instead

If child support is not being paid, there are legal options to protect your rights without putting your case—or your child—at risk.

Enforce the support order. A motion to enforce allows the court to address unpaid support through wage withholding, tax interception, or other remedies.

Work with a family law attorney. An experienced attorney can help document payments properly and pursue enforcement without exposing you to allegations of noncompliance.

Keep the focus on your child. Continuing to follow visitation orders demonstrates responsibility and cooperation, both of which courts take seriously when resolving disputes.

The Real Takeaway

It is frustrating when a parent doesn't pay child support, but two wrongs do not make a right, and they rarely lead to good outcomes. Texas law enforcers handle child support and visitation separately because both are considered essential to a child's well-being. If your ex is not paying for support, do not take matters into your own hands. Take them to court the right way, with the right help.

CHAPTER 9:

Myth #6:
If I Do not Want the Divorce, I Can Stop It

"I didn't agree to this, so it shouldn't be able to happen, right?"

One of the most painful situations I see is when divorce papers blindside a spouse. They believed things were fixable, or they weren't told a filing was coming until they were actually being served. Shock turns into anger, confusion, and the hope that refusing to participate will somehow pause the process. Unfortunately, that is not how divorce works in Texas.

The Short Answer

No, you cannot stop a divorce simply because you disagree with it. Texas law does not require mutual consent to end a marriage. Once one spouse files for divorce and meets the legal requirements, the court will proceed whether the other spouse wants to proceed or not. Texas is a no-fault divorce state. A spouse may seek divorce by alleging that the marriage has become insupportable under Texas Family Code § 6.001. No proof of wrongdoing is required.

Why This Myth Causes Real Harm

This myth often traps people in denial during the most critical phase of a case. Believing that simply disagreeing with what is happening can stop the divorce altogether leads some people to ignore paperwork, delay hiring an attorney, or avoid responding to their spouse's lawyer. Meanwhile, deadlines are not adjusted. Hearings are scheduled. Decisions are made. Sometimes, those decisions are made whether or not both spouses are present, to protect themselves.

Waiting does not stop a divorce. It only puts you behind.

What Texas Law Actually Allows

There are a few realities about divorce proceedings that surprise many people.

- Only one spouse needs to file for divorce in Texas.
- Fault is optional. Most divorces proceed on no-fault grounds.
- You do not have to sign divorce papers for the divorce to be finalized.

If a spouse is served and fails to respond within the required time frame—typically twenty days—the court may grant a **default judgment**. That means the filing spouse can receive many of the outcomes they requested without opposition.

What Happens If You Do Nothing

If you choose not to respond because you disagree with the divorce, the case does not stop. The court proceeds, your spouse may seek a default judgment, and your voice may never be heard. This is how people lose property, parenting time, and financial protection. This is not because the law was applied unfairly, but because they didn't participate.

What You Should Do Instead

Even if you do not want a divorce, you still have the right and the responsibility to protect yourself.

Respond to the petition. Filing a response preserves your rights, even if reconciliation is still possible.

Get legal advice early on. An attorney can explain your options, help you meet deadlines, and prevent a default judgment that could leave you with an outcome you never agreed to.

Stay involved. Being proactive allows you to influence custody, property division, and financial outcomes.

The Real Takeaway

Being forced into a divorce is deeply painful, but refusing to engage will not stop the process. That only leaves you unprotected because Texas law allows one spouse to end a marriage. You may not be able to stop divorce from happening, but you can absolutely influence how it turns out.

CHAPTER 10:

Myth #7: Moving Out of the Marital Home Means Giving Up Rights to It

This myth usually reemerges when the tension at home becomes unbearable and someone packs a bag just to get some space.

Then a well-meaning friend says, "If you move out, you give up your rights to the house."

A choice made for peace now seems legally wrong.

To be clear, in Texas, moving out of the marital home does not mean you lose ownership interest. But, like many things in divorce, the consequences depend on how and why you move.

The Short Answer

No, moving out of the marital home does not automatically mean that you forfeit your rights to it. Texas is a community property state. If the home was purchased during the marriage, it is generally presumed to be community property, regardless of whose name is on the deed or who remains in the house for the duration of the divorce proceedings.

Moving out may impact temporary custody and possession arrangements in your case.

How Texas Courts View the Marital Home

If a home was acquired during the marriage, both spouses usually have a financial interest in it. That remains true even if one spouse moves out during the divorce. So, when courts eventually decide what happens to the home, they focus on overall fairness, not on who stayed and who left. To this end, judges may consider:

- The length of the marriage
- Each spouse's financial contributions
- Post-divorce housing needs
- Custody arrangements and a child's need for stability

What Moving Out Can Affect

While moving out does not eliminate ownership rights, it can influence other parts of the case.

Temporary custody and stability: if children remain at home with one parent, courts may view that arrangement as more stable in the short term. Judges often try to minimize disruption for children when issuing temporary orders.

Temporary possession of the home: a court may grant one spouse exclusive use of the home while the divorce is pending as a temporary measure, not necessarily a final determination of ownership.

Financial obligations: moving out does not necessarily terminate one's responsibility for the mortgage, taxes, or upkeep, especially if the home is community property or both spouses are on the loan.

How to Protect Yourself If You Are Considering Moving Out

Leaving the home does not render your rights null and void, but how you leave matters.

Get legal advice first. Before moving out, speak with a family law attorney. Timing, safety, parenting schedules, and financial considerations all matter in these kinds of cases.

Document your financial contributions. Keep records of mortgage payments, repairs, taxes, and insurance. Documentation safeguards your finances.

Seek temporary orders when appropriate. Temporary court orders can clarify possession, custody, and financial responsibilities, not to mention prevent misunderstandings while the case is still pending.

The Real Takeaway

You are not punished simply for leaving the marital home, but moving out without a plan can create avoidable complications. In Texas, ownership is not determined by who stayed, but by what is fair under the law. If you are considering moving out, do not panic or make uneducated guesses as to what to do next. With planning and sound legal advice, you can protect your rights and your peace.

CHAPTER 11:

Myth #8: You Can Avoid Paying Child Support by Quitting Your Job or Taking One That Pays Less

"I will just quit my job or get one that pays less. Then I won't owe as much child support."

It sounds simple, but it doesn't work in Texas, or in most states. It certainly does not work in the eyes of a family court judge.

The Short Answer

No, you cannot avoid paying for child support by voluntarily reducing your income. Child support is a legal obligation, not a suggestion. It exists to protect children by ensuring they have food, housing, education, and health care. If a court suspects a parent is intentionally under-earning to lower support payments, it can intervene directly.

What Happens When Income Is Voluntarily Reduced

Texas courts look beyond paychecks. They look at earning capacity.

Income can be imputed. If a judge determines that a parent is intentionally unemployed or underemployed, the court may assign or impute income based on what that parent is reasonably capable of earning. Support is then calculated using that figure, not their current earnings. In short, reducing your income on paper does not reduce your obligation in the eyes of the court.

Enforcement tools are serious. When you try to avoid paying for support, courts can enforce these orders through wage garnishment, interception of tax refunds, suspension of driver's or professional licenses, liens on property or bank accounts, and contempt proceedings that may result in fines or jail time.

Custody can be affected. Judges expect parents to act responsibly. Attempts to avoid financial obligations may raise concerns about judgment and responsibility, which can affect custody or visitation decisions.

A Practical Example

Imagine a professional who earns $120,000 per year suddenly quits and takes a part-time job earning $15,000 shortly after a divorce has been filed. If the court believes the change was strategic rather than necessary, child support will likely be calculated based on what that parent should be earning, not on what they chose to earn in their new position. The obligation doesn't disappear; it simply becomes enforceable at a higher level.

Why This Strategy Backfires

Trying to dodge child support almost always makes things worse because it undermines one's credibility with the court, invites aggressive enforcement, and harms the children that the support is meant to protect. Judges take child support seriously, so attempted gamesmanship in this area rarely ends well.

What to Do If Your Income Drops Legitimately

Life happens. Jobs are lost. Illness occurs. Industries change. So, when your income drops for legitimate reasons, the right approach is transparency, not avoidance.

File for modification promptly. If your circumstances change, request a review of your support order as soon as possible.

Get legal guidance. An experienced family law attorney can help properly document changes and present them in a way the court will take seriously.

Stay focused on the children involved. Acting in good faith, staying engaged, and remaining cooperative go a long way in both legal and personal capacities.

The Real Takeaway

Quitting your job or earning less doesn't help you avoid paying child support. In fact, it usually creates a bigger problem for you. Texas courts are equipped to identify and correct attempts to evade support obligations. The better path is honesty, prompt action, and focusing on what support is intended to do, which is to protect your children.

CHAPTER 12:

Myth #9:
Men Always End Up Paying Spousal Support

"I will probably have to pay spousal support, right? That's just how it goes."

Not necessarily. In fact, the belief that men always pay spousal support is one of the most outdated misconceptions in modern family law.

The Short Answer

No, men do not always pay spousal support. In Texas, spousal support (also called spousal maintenance) is not based on gender. It is based on financial need, disparity in earning capacity, and the specific facts related to the marriage. Courts are not interested in stereotypes, but fairness.

How Spousal Maintenance Works in Texas

Under Texas Family Code §8.051, spousal maintenance is awarded only when certain statutory conditions are met. It is not automatic, and it is not common. When courts evaluate whether spousal maintenance is appropriate, they consider several factors.

Length of the marriage: Longer marriages (typically ten or more years) are more likely to qualify, particularly when one spouse has been financially dependent on the other.

Financial resources: the court considers whether the requesting spouse can meet minimum reasonable needs after the divorce, not whether they are accustomed to a particular lifestyle.

Earning capacity and sacrifices: if one spouse gave up education, training, or career advancement opportunities to support the household or raise the children, that sacrifice matters.

Contributions to marriage: contributions such as homemaking or caregiving are given real weight even though they are not considered financial ones.

Misconduct: In some cases, violence or financial misconduct may affect one's eligibility or the amount of maintenance that will ultimately be ordered.

What the Court Does Not Consider

Historically, women received spousal support more often because traditional household roles placed men as primary earners. That reality has changed, so gender is no longer a given deciding factor. Today:

- If a wife earns significantly more than her husband, she may be ordered to pay maintenance.
- If both spouses are financially independent, neither may owe the other support.

- If the spouse earning less is male, he has the right to request maintenance.

Clearing Up Common Misconceptions

Spousal support is not guaranteed. Most divorces in Texas do not result in any maintenance at all, and when maintenance is awarded, it is rarely permanent. When awarded, spousal maintenance is usually temporary and designed to help the receiving spouse regain financial independence. It is never automatic, as every case is evaluated based on its own facts.

A Practical Example

Consider a couple that's been married for twelve years. The wife earns $160,000 per year. The husband has been a stay-at-home parent for almost ten years, without full-time employment. If they divorce, the husband may qualify for temporary spousal maintenance while he rebuilds his career. The deciding factors here are income disparity and financial dependence, not gender.

The Real Takeaway

Spousal support in Texas is about need, resources, and fairness, not tradition or assumptions. If you are a man facing divorce, do not assume you will automatically be ordered to pay support. If you are a woman who earns more, understand that fairness applies both ways.

Courts do not ask, "Who is the husband or the wife?" They ask, "Who needs support, and who can provide it?"

CHAPTER 13:

Myth #10: You Do not Need a Lawyer in an Amicable Divorce

Many couples begin the divorce proceedings under the belief that if they are getting along, they can avoid lawyers altogether. They agree on the big issues, want to keep things peaceful, and worry that involving attorneys will only complicate matters.

That belief is understandable, but it is also one of the most common mistakes I see. Even the most amicable divorce is still a legal proceeding, and skipping legal guidance often creates problems that arise much later, when they are far more expensive and difficult to fix.

The Short Answer

Yes, you still need a lawyer, even in an amicable divorce. Amicable does not mean simple; divorce requires compliance with Texas law, the proper filing of documents, enforceable agreements, and court approval. When those items aren't handled correctly, good intentions do not prevent bad outcomes.

Why Legal Guidance Still Matters

Even cooperative divorces involve legal complexity.

Understanding the law: Texas has specific rules governing property division, spousal maintenance, and child custody. An attorney ensures that agreements comply with the law and will be accepted by the court.

Drafting enforceable agreements: informal or poorly drafted agreements may feel sufficient at the time, but can be vague, unenforceable, or incomplete in the eyes of the court. Ambiguity often invites conflict later on.

Catching overlooked issues: friendly couples often overlook important details such as tax consequences, division of retirement accounts, health insurance coverage, and future support obligations.

Preventing future disputes: properly drafted divorce decrees anticipate change. Lawyers include provisions for modification, enforcement, and dispute resolution that help prevent a cooperative divorce from turning contentious.

How Lawyers Often Preserve Peace

Contrary to popular belief, hiring a lawyer does not automatically turn an amicable divorce into a fight. In fact, skilled attorneys often help couples:

- Communicate clearly and avoid misunderstandings
- Stay focused on shared goals rather than the emotions of the individual
- Resolve small disagreements before they escalate

Most people do not need courtroom warriors. They need steady guidance and clear drafting.

A Practical Example

I often see couples agree to split retirement accounts without using a Qualified Domestic Relations Order (a QDRO). Years later, one spouse discovers they never received their share, and fixing the mistake costs far more than proper legal guidance would have in the first place. That kind of problem doesn't come from conflict, but from incomplete planning.

The Real Takeaway

A lawyer doesn't turn an amicable divorce into a war. A lawyer helps ensure that a peaceful separation remains peaceful and enforceable. Even in an uncontested divorce, legal guidance helps:

- Protect your rights
- Finalize binding, thorough agreements
- Avoid costly mistakes that surface later

Closing the Myths

And with that, we have addressed the ten most common divorce myths I hear from clients across Texas. If you have read this far, you have already taken an important step in replacing fear and misinformation with understanding.

Divorce is never easy, but it doesn't have to be chaotic, punishing, or confusing. Informed decisions lead to better results for families and their future.

The rest of this book will focus on the process, the strategy involved in divorce proceedings, and how to move forward with clarity and confidence.

CHAPTER 14:

Understanding Divorce in Texas

If you are considering divorce, you are not alone. And for many people, divorce marks a painful transition. For others, however, it is a turning point, a step toward stability, clarity, and, eventually, a more secure future. Either way, divorce is rarely easy. It is a complex, emotionally charged process that affects far more than paperwork. Not knowing what comes next can make it that much harder to get through.

The good news is that when people understand how divorce works in Texas, fear loses much of its power. With the right information and the right support, you can approach this process with clarity, confidence, and control. This section of the book is designed to give you that solid foundation.

Why Understanding the Process Matters

I've seen people make costly mistakes simply because they didn't understand how divorce unfolds in the real world. They reacted emotionally, relied on misinformation, or assumed the worst, and those assumptions shaped their decisions.

Understanding the process doesn't make divorce painless, but it does make it manageable. When you know what the law requires, how courts evaluate individual cases, and what steps lie ahead, you can make deliberate choices instead of reactive ones and make better outcomes more likely.

The Short Answer

If you are considering divorce in Texas, you need to understand three things:

- How the legal process works
- What the law requires of you
- How to protect yourself legally, financially, and emotionally

This chapter—and those that follow—are your roadmap. I will break down Texas divorce law in plain language, without unnecessary legal jargon or scare tactics. You'll learn how the system works and where people most often go wrong. Specifically, we'll cover:

- Residency requirements and eligibility to file in Texas
- What happens after a divorce petition is filed
- Temporary orders involving custody, property, and financial support
- How courts evaluate custody, property division, and spousal maintenance
- Why legal guidance matters even in amicable or uncontested divorces

The goal is not to turn you into a lawyer, but to help you stop guessing about what you should do next. We'll start with the divorce process itself—from filing to final orders—so you understand the timeline and what each stage entails. Then, we'll discuss fault versus no-fault divorce and how behavior can affect outcomes. From there, we'll shift into strategy and proof, which references how courts make decisions, what evidence matters, and how credibility is built or lost. We'll also take a closer look at custody, property division, and spousal support, followed by how to choose the right attorney and work with them every step of the way.

Each chapter builds on the last. You do not have to read them all at once, but taken together, they can give you a clear picture of what you are facing.

Moving Forward with Clarity

Divorce can feel overwhelming, especially at the beginning, but going through it blindly can cause the most damage. The more you understand, the more control you have. Whether your goal is to protect your relationships with your children, secure your financial future, or simply understand your options, this section is here to help you move forward deliberately, not fearfully.

CHAPTER 15:

The Divorce Process in Texas

Divorce is a word loaded with emotion. Fear, frustration, grief, relief—and yes, sometimes hope—all tend to be associated with it, and sometimes all at once. Whether you are the one initiating the divorce or simply trying to respond, the process can feel overwhelming. Texas divorce law has its own rules, timelines, and procedural requirements, and most people encounter them for the first time when they are already under the stress of pending separation.

This chapter explains the process so you can proceed confidently.

Starting a Divorce in Texas

Every divorce in Texas starts the same way: with the filing of a **Petition for Divorce**.

Before a case can be filed, certain residency requirements must be met. At least one spouse must have lived in Texas for at least six months and in the county where the case is filed for at least ninety days.

Once the petition is filed, it sets out two things: the legal grounds for divorce and the issues the court is being asked to decide, such as property division, child custody, or spousal support. The other spouse must then be formally served with the petition and given an opportunity to respond. If they do, the case proceeds normally. If no response is filed, the court may eventually allow a default judgment, meaning the case moves forward without the unresponsive spouse's input.

Temporary Orders: Stabilizing the Situation

Due to lengthy divorce proceedings, Texas courts commonly issue temporary orders at the start of cases. These are designed to provide structure and stability while the divorce is pending. Temporary orders may pertain to the following matters:

- Who remains in the marital home
- Temporary custody and visitation schedules
- Temporary child or spousal support
- Use of vehicles, accounts, or other shared property

These orders are not permanent; they simply exist to prevent chaos and conflict while the case moves toward resolution.

The Core Issues in Every Divorce

Every divorce is unique, but in my experience, most Texas divorces revolve around three central issues.

Property division: Texas is a community property state, which means that most assets and debts acquired during the marriage presumably belong to both spouses. Courts divide community property in a manner that is just and right, considering factors such as earning capacity, contributions to marriage, future needs, and, in some cases, fault.

Child custody and support: custody decisions are guided by what is in the child's best interest. Parents are encouraged to agree on a parenting plan, but if they cannot, the judge will decide based on each parent's involvement, stability, and ability to meet the child's needs. Support is calculated using statutory guidelines like income, number of children, and parenting time.

Spousal support: spousal support, or spousal maintenance, is not automatic in Texas. Courts evaluate whether a spouse can take care of minimum reasonable needs after the divorce based on factors such as the length of the marriage, earning capacity, and financial disparity.

Fault Versus No-Fault Divorce

Texas allows both fault-based and no-fault divorces. Most divorces cite insupportability as no-fault grounds. Fault-based grounds—such as adultery or cruelty—must be proven, and even then do not automatically change outcomes.

Do All Divorces Go to Trial?

Most Texas divorces are resolved through negotiation, mediation, or settlement. These approaches are often faster, less expensive, and less emotionally draining than courtroom litigation. Trials are necessary only when disputes cannot be resolved by agreement. In those cases, a judge decides the unresolved issues based on evidence and the law.

Why Legal Guidance Matters

Even in cooperative divorces, problems can arise quickly and cause long-term damage: missed deadlines, incomplete paperwork, unclear agreements, and unintended financial consequences. Legal guidance helps ensure that:

- Deadlines are met
- Documents are filed correctly
- Agreements are enforceable
- Long-term consequences are considered

The goal is not to create conflict, but to prevent avoidable mistakes.

The Real Takeaway

Divorce is both a legal process and an emotional journey. Feeling overwhelmed at the beginning is normal; what matters is how you respond to that uncertainty.

When you understand the process, you regain control. When you stop guessing, you make better decisions. And when you move deliberately instead of reactively, outcomes improve.

CHAPTER 16:

Fault Versus No-Fault Divorce in Texas

One of the first questions people ask me when considering divorce is deceptively simple.

"Should I file for a fault divorce or a no-fault divorce?"

At first, that distinction can sound like legal jargon. In reality, it can influence how certain parts of your case unfold, particularly property division, custody, and spousal support. Understanding the difference helps you make a strategic decision instead of an emotional one.

The Short Answer

A no-fault divorce means the marriage has become insupportable. In other words, it is broken beyond repair, and no one is to blame in a legal sense. On the other hand, a fault-based divorce means one spouse is alleging that the other's misconduct caused the breakdown of the marriage. This can refer to adultery, cruelty, or abandonment. And yes, the distinction can matter.

How Texas Law Defines Each

No-fault divorce: under Texas Family Code §6.001, a divorce may be granted when the marriage has become insupportable due to conflict or discord that destroys the legitimate ends of the relationship. No proof of wrongdoing is required. Most divorces in Texas proceed on this basis.

Fault-based divorce: terms of a divorce can also be based on specific grounds listed in Texas Family Code §§6.002–6.007, including adultery, cruelty, abandonment, felony conviction, living apart for at least three years, or confinement in a mental institution. In fault-based cases, the spouse making the allegation must present evidence to support their claims.

Why the Choice Matters

Filing on fault grounds does not automatically change the outcome of a divorce, but in some situations, it can influence how certain issues are resolved.

Property division: Texas is a community property state, but courts divide property in a manner that is just and right. If a spouse shows that the other's misconduct, like marital waste or hiding assets, harmed their shared estate, the court may grant them a larger share of property.

Child custody: fault can matter if it directly affects a child's safety or well-being. Abuse, neglect, or endangerment may influence custody decisions. A fault that has no impact on the child usually does not.

Spousal support: In limited situations, misconduct (particularly family violence or financial abuse) may affect eligibility for spousal maintenance or the amount that is ultimately awarded.

Choosing Between Fault and No-Fault Proceedings

No-fault divorce is simpler and more common. Most cases proceed this way because it avoids the expense, stress, and evidentiary burden of proving misconduct. It allows the case to move forward without turning the divorce into a trial about who is to blame.

Fault-based divorce can be strategic—in the right case. If misconduct had a real impact on finances, affected parenting decisions, or created safety concerns, pursuing fault may make sense. But it comes with tradeoffs: longer timelines, higher costs, and greater emotional strain.

A Word of Caution

Proving fault often feels emotionally satisfying, but it rarely delivers the dramatic legal advantage people expect. Unless the facts are serious, documented, and legally relevant, fault claims simply intensify conflict without meaningfully improving anyone's outcome. That's why this decision should be made carefully, not reactively.

The Real Takeaway

You do not need to prove wrongdoing to get divorced in Texas. In many cases, no-fault divorce is the most efficient and effective path forward.

That said, fault can matter in specific circumstances. The key is understanding when it helps, and when it doesn't. An experienced family law attorney can help you evaluate:

- The strength of available evidence
- The cost and emotional impact of litigation
- Whether fault is likely to influence property, custody, or support

The goal is not to assign blame, but to choose the strategy that best protects your future.

CHAPTER 17:

You Are at War, But It is a War That Can Be Won

Divorce is a battle, just not in the sense of violence or destruction. It can be in terms of stakes, strategy, and endurance. There are moments when it feels like everything is on the line: your finances, your children, your reputation, and your future. When emotions run high and things begin to feel uncertain, it is easy to make decisions out of fear instead of with intention.

I want you to understand that this is a war you can win, and winning does not mean destroying the other side.

What Winning Actually Means

In family law, winning is not about humiliation or punishment. It is about protection and stability.

- Protecting your relationships with your children
- Preserving your financial future
- Maintaining your credibility with the court
- Building a life for after the divorce is finalized

Those who come out of divorce at their strongest are not the most aggressive, but the better prepared.

Strategy Beats Emotion Every Time

In my experience, divorce is not won through anger or impulse, but through strategy and evidence. Favorable outcomes come from understanding what matters legally and focusing your energy there. Whether your case involves custody, property, or spousal support, success depends on preparation, not volume. That preparation includes:

- Documenting finances accurately
- Preserving relevant evidence
- Proposing reasonable, lawful solutions
- Communicating through appropriate legal channels

When people abandon strategy for emotion, they usually lose ground they never get back.

You Do not Have to Fight Alone

Can someone technically represent themselves in a divorce? Yes, but doing so is like walking into a complex negotiation without understanding the rules, the typical timeline, or the consequences of a significant misstep. Even people with the best intentions make irreversible mistakes when they try to manage this process alone. An experienced divorce attorney serves as a buffer between your emotions and your decision-making abilities. Their goal is not to escalate conflict, but to:

- Protect rights and assets
- Ensure deadlines are met, and procedures are followed

- Negotiate from a position of strength rather than reactive emotions
- Make sure agreements are enforceable and that they consider future obstacles or situations

Even in straightforward or noncombative cases, legal guidance is often what keeps things amicable.

Lessons From the Front Lines

Over the years, I've seen people approach divorce in two destructive ways. Some try to "stay civil" without legal guidance and later realize that they gave up far more than they had intended to. Others treat divorce as personal warfare and end up damaging their own credibility, finances, or even their relationships with their children. The best outcomes come from balance.

- Firm, but fair
- Assertive, not aggressive
- Protective, not punitive

This balance is where strategy lives.

The Real Takeaway

You do not have to become someone you are not in order to get through a divorce. You do not have to be ruthless or passive, and you do not have to fight every battle. You do need to be informed, deliberate, and supported. Divorce is a war, but it can be won through preparation, clarity, and sound decision-making. When you approach it that way, survival often turns into something better: stability, confidence, and a future you can move toward without regret.

CHAPTER 18:

What Must You Prove to Win Your Case

If you are in the middle of a divorce or preparing for one, you may ask a very practical question.

"How do I actually win this?"

The answer is not just hiring a good lawyer, although that does matter. Winning comes from presenting the right evidence, in the right way, at the right time.

The Short Answer

Winning your case means building a clear, credible narrative supported by facts, not emotions. Judges decide cases based on admissible evidence and legal standards. The more organized your proof is, the stronger your position will be.

Know What You are Trying to Prove

Before gathering evidence, you need to understand what the court is evaluating.

Child custody decisions are governed by the child's best interests under Texas Family Code §153.002. Relevant evidence may include:

- Parenting schedules and involvement
- Communication records
- School and medical records
- Testimony from teachers, counselors, or family members

Property division must be executed in a manner that is just and right. Evidence often decides:

- What is separate versus community property
- Financial and non-financial contributions
- Any conduct that harmed the marital estate

Spousal support must be determined or opposed through evidence, which may include:

- Inability to meet basic needs
- Lack of capacity to earn
- Career sacrifices during marriage
- Disability or full-time caregiving responsibilities

Gathering the Right Evidence

Evidence is the backbone of your legal strategy. Without it, arguments are just opinions. Common forms of evidence include:

- Financial records such as bank statements, tax returns, and pay stubs
- Text messages or emails related to parenting, finances, or misconduct

- Photos or videos of assets, their conditions, or each spouse's involvement with them
- Expert testimony from psychologists, accountants, or evaluators
- Witness testimony from people with direct knowledge of the circumstances

Your attorney's role is to ensure this evidence is admissible and presented effectively.

Credibility Is a Legal Asset

Even strong evidence can fall flat if a judge doesn't trust the person who presents it. Credibility is built by:

- Being truthful, even when it is uncomfortable
- Following court orders and meeting deadlines
- Remaining respectful during hearings and mediation
- Avoiding inflammatory social media activity
- Always being professional

Judges notice behavioral patterns. Credibility can quietly close cases.

Anticipating the Other Side

Divorce is adversarial by nature. Expect resistance. Winning often requires:

- Understanding the other side's strongest arguments
- Identifying vulnerabilities in your own position
- Neutralizing unreliable or exaggerated claims
- Responding with evidence instead of emotion

A strong strategy doesn't just tell your story; it prevents the other side's from overtaking it.

You and Your Attorney's Respective Roles

Your attorney handles legal strategy, evidence, and courtroom procedure. Your role is to:

- Stay organized
- Be honest
- Respond promptly
- Follow advice
- Keep long-term goals in focus

The strongest cases come from collaboration, not conflict.

The Real Takeaway

Winning your divorce case doesn't require theatrics. Rather, it requires preparation, proof, and credibility. You do not need a perfect story. You need to prove the truth of yours more effectively than the other side proves the reality of theirs.

CHAPTER 19:

Child Custody, Property Division, and Spousal Support

Divorce in Texas involves far more than ending a marriage. It determines where children will live, how property will be divided, and whether one spouse will provide financial support to the other. Divorce decisions affect lives well beyond finalization.

Understanding how courts approach all of this gives you the clarity you need to make informed decisions with your future in mind, rather than react out of fear or uncertainty.

Child Custody in Texas

Custody is often the most emotionally charged part of a divorce. It determines not only where a child lives, but who makes major decisions about education, health care, and upbringing. Texas law divides custody into two components:

- Conservatorship (legal custody): decision-making authority
- Possession and access (physical custody): parenting time

Texas courts strongly prefer that both parents remain involved in a child's life. In most cases, judges appoint **joint managing**

conservators unless there is evidence of abuse, neglect, or serious conflict that would endanger the child.

When deciding custody, courts focus on stability, not gender. Judges consider factors such as:

- The child's age, health, and emotional needs
- Each parent's ability to provide a stable environment
- History of caregiving and involvement
- Any history of family violence, substance abuse, or neglect

Custody decisions are guided by what is in the child's best interest. When parents cannot agree on that, courts may appoint a mediator, a guardian ad litem, or a custody evaluator to make recommendations.

Property Division in Texas

Texas is a community property state, meaning most property acquired during the marriage is presumed to belong to both spouses. That does not mean everything is divided equally. Courts divide community property in the right manner, according to Texas Family Code §7.001. Fairness, not symmetry, is the goal. Key concepts include the following.

- Community property: wages, retirement accounts, real estate, vehicles, and debts acquired during the marriage.
- Separate property: assets owned before marriage, inheritances, and gifts if they come with documentation.

When dividing property, courts may consider:

- Each spouse's earning capacity
- Financial and non-financial contributions
- Fault that harmed the marital estate
- Custody arrangements and future needs
- The size of each spouse's separate estate

Property division becomes more complex when businesses, retirement accounts, or real estate are involved, and when assets have been commingled over time.

Spousal Support in Texas

Spousal support is not automatic and is only awarded in limited circumstances. Courts evaluate if a spouse can meet minimum reasonable needs after the divorce. Maintenance, which is usually temporary and intended to help a spouse regain financial independence, may be considered if:

- The marriage lasted ten years or more, and one spouse lacks earning capacity
- A spouse is caring for a disabled child
- A spouse is physically or mentally disabled
- Family violence occurred within two years of filing

Courts also evaluate:

- The length of the marriage
- Employment history and job skills

- Educational background
- Career sacrifices made during the marriage
- Financial misconduct

Spousal maintenance may be ordered as monthly payments or, in limited cases, as a lump sum.

The Bigger Picture

Custody, property division, and spousal support are not isolated decisions. They interact with one another to shape long-term stability for both parents and children because divorce is not just about resolving the past. It is about building a foundation for the future. Every case is different, so understanding how courts approach these issues is essential before making decisions that can't easily be undone.

The Real Takeaway

Divorce outcomes are shaped by preparation, clarity, and informed decision-making, not panic or assumptions. When you understand how custody, property, and support actually work, you are better positioned to protect what matters most and move forward deliberately.

CHAPTER 20:

Do You Need an Attorney for Your Divorce?

Divorce is expensive. When people face court fees, housing changes, and uncertainty about the future, it is natural to wonder whether they can feasibly avoid hiring a lawyer.

"I can probably handle this myself."

"It seems simple enough."

"We're getting along; lawyers will just complicate things."

I understand why people think that way. Unfortunately, those assumptions are often what create the most expensive problems later. The fact is that divorce is not just an emotional process. It is a legal one, and legal mistakes tend to surface long after the paperwork is signed, and when they are much harder to fix.

The Short Answer

Yes, you really do need a divorce attorney, even if your case seems simple, if it starts amicably, or if the communication between you and your spouse is still civil. The biggest risk in divorce is not conflict; it is misunderstanding what you agree to.

Why Legal Representation Matters

Divorce law is detailed and unforgiving. Texas Family Code governs everything from how property is divided to how custody orders must be written and enforced. Missing a requirement or deadline, or relying on informal agreements, can have permanent consequences.

Over the years, I've seen people lose property rights, parenting time, or financial protections, and not because they were unreasonable, but because they didn't realize what the law required.

Mistakes in Divorce Are Expensive

Do-it-yourself divorces often fail in predictable ways:

- Missed filing deadlines
- Incomplete or unenforceable agreements
- Overlooked tax consequences
- Improper division of retirement accounts
- Vague custody provisions that eventually invite conflict

Fixing those mistakes later often costs far more than doing it correctly in the beginning.

Lawyers Do More than Go to Court

Many people assume hiring a lawyer means preparing for a fight. In reality, experienced family law attorneys spend far more time preventing conflict than creating it. A good attorney helps:

- Keep negotiations focused and productive
- Draft clear, enforceable agreements

- Anticipate future issues before they arise
- Protect your interests without escalating tension

Lawyers do not cause conflict. They manage it.

Emotion Clouds Judgment, but Lawyers Restore Perspective

Divorce brings on fear, anger, grief, and guilt. Those emotions are normal, but they can also be dangerous when legal decisions are involved. An attorney provides distance and perspective, and that objectivity often prevents decisions that feel right in the moment but cause regret later.

One Lawyer Cannot Represent Both Spouses.

Even in amicable divorces, one attorney cannot ethically represent both sides. Someone must be focused solely on your rights, your goals, and your future.

That doesn't mean your divorce has to become adversarial. It means that you are protected.

What Happens When People Skip Legal Guidance

When people move forward without legal advice, the risks are real:

- Unequal property division
- Overpaying or under-receiving support
- Poorly drafted custody orders
- Problems enforcing stipulations years later

The most painful part is that many do not realize anything is wrong until it is too late to change.

Choosing the Right Attorney Matters

Not all lawyers are the same. When selecting a divorce attorney, experience in family law, communication style, transparency, and judgment matter more than aggression or promises. The right attorney helps you navigate the process strategically and keeps the focus on long-term stability.

The Real Takeaway

You wouldn't perform surgery on yourself. You wouldn't represent yourself in a criminal case. You wouldn't close a complex real estate transaction without guidance. Divorce is no different. Hiring an attorney is not an admission of failure, but an investment in clarity, protection, and your peace of mind.

CHAPTER 21:

Finding a Qualified Divorce Lawyer

Divorce is emotional, legal, and personal. The attorney you choose will help shape some of the most important aspects of your life: finances, your relationships with your children, and your overall stability. This is not a decision you want to rush into or make based on convenience. You need someone who understands Texas divorce law and you. This chapter can help you choose wisely.

Why the Right Lawyer Matters

A good divorce attorney is more than someone who files paperwork. They become your advocate, strategist, and protector at a time when emotions can cloud judgment. The right lawyer helps you:

- Avoid costly mistakes
- Navigate custody, property, and support issues confidently
- Mitigate unnecessary conflict
- Work toward the best possible outcome through settlement or court

Not every lawyer is built for family law, and not every family law attorney is right for every client.

Where to Start Your Search

Many people begin with referrals, and that's a reasonable place to start. Friends or family members who have been through a divorce can share insight about their experience, such as what they valued and what they would do differently. That being said, your case is unique, and the lawyer who worked well for someone else may not be the best fit for you.

Another useful resource is the State Bar of Texas, which offers a referral service that lets you confirm whether an attorney is licensed and in good standing. Reputable legal directories can also provide helpful background information, including practice focus and client feedback.

What to Look for in a Divorce Attorney

Experience matters, particularly in Texas family law. As you evaluate potential attorneys, ask practical questions.

- Do they focus primarily on family law?
- How familiar are they with cases like yours?
- Have they handled custody disputes, complex property division, or other issues relevant to your situation?

Membership in professional organizations, peer recognition, or board certification can indicate commitment to the field, but they are not substitutes for sound judgment and real-world experience.

The Consultation Matters More Than You Think

A consultation is your opportunity to assess more than an attorney's credentials. It is a chance to determine whether their approach aligns with your needs. Ask about:

- Experience with cases similar to yours
- Communication style and availability
- If their strategy tends to be collaborative, firm, or a balance of both
- Fee structure and billing practices

Bring relevant documents if you have them, and pay attention to how clearly your questions are answered. Trust your instincts; comfort and communication matter.

Compatibility and Communication Are Essential

Your attorney will help you make decisions that affect your future. You should feel comfortable being honest and asking questions, even the most difficult ones. Before hiring anyone, ask yourself:

- Do I feel heard and respected?
- Are their explanations clear and straightforward?
- Can I trust this person to tell me the truth, even when it is uncomfortable?

If the answer to these questions is yes, you are likely on the right track.

Discuss Fees Up Front

Clarifying fees from the beginning can prevent frustration later. Divorce attorneys in Texas typically bill hourly and require a retainer up front. Some matters may qualify for flat fees, particularly in uncontested cases. Before moving forward, make sure you understand:

- How billing works
- How often invoices are issued
- What happens if the retainer is exhausted

A Final Word on Choosing Wisely

Finding the right divorce lawyer is one of the most important decisions you'll make during this process. They bring legal knowledge, perspective, strategy, and calm when you need it most. Do not rush the decision. Ask thoughtful questions. Choose someone you can trust to guide you through this transition with professionalism and care.

CHAPTER 22:

What Does an Experienced Divorce Lawyer Do for You?

There are rules you do not know, deadlines you won't expect, and decisions that lead to long-term consequences. Trying to navigate that process alone often leads to confusion, stress, and costly mistakes.

An experienced divorce lawyer does more than filing paperwork. They provide structure, strategy, and protection during one of the most demanding periods of your life. Here's what that looks like in practice.

Clear Guidance Through a Complex Process

Texas divorce law is detailed and procedural. From custody rules to community property classifications, to filing requirements, even small mistakes can have serious repercussions. An experienced attorney helps by:

- Explaining the law in plain language
- Clarifying your rights and responsibilities
- Identifying risks early on in the process
- Developing a strategy that's tailored to your goals

Instead of reacting to problems as they arise, they will guide you through the process with intention.

Strategic Negotiation Without Escalation

Every divorce involves negotiation, even those that never go to trial. Parenting time, property division, and support arrangements all require compromise. A skilled lawyer knows how to:

- Negotiate directly with opposing counsel
- Advocate firmly without escalating conflict
- Recognize when to push and when to compromise
- Protect your long-term interests, not just the short-term wins

Effective negotiation prevents unnecessary battles and preserves both financial and emotional resources.

Advocacy When Court Becomes Necessary

Most divorces settle, but some do not. When a trial is unavoidable, having an attorney who understands courtroom procedure and judicial expectations is critical. Your lawyer becomes your advocate, acting clearly and persuasively to ensure your position is properly represented. That includes:

- Preparing and presenting evidence
- Examining and cross-examining witnesses
- Arguing motions and dissecting legal issues
- Framing your case in a way that judges understand and respect

The court is not about theatrics. It is about preparation, credibility, and proof.

Managing the Paperwork and the Procedures

Divorce involves extensive documentation: pleadings, financial disclosures, orders, deadlines, and court communications. Errors in paperwork can delay a case or undermine your legal position. An experienced attorney:

- Prepares and files documents correctly
- Tracks deadlines and procedural requirements
- Handles service and court communications
- Ensure orders are enforceable and complete

Attention to detail protects your case and allows you to focus on rebuilding, not just paperwork.

Stability During an Emotional Process

Divorce is not only legal; it is emotional. And while an attorney is not a therapist, a good lawyer provides perspective when emotions threaten to drive your decisions. They help you slow down, consider consequences, and stay focused on the future. That steady guidance often prevents clients from making decisions out of fear, anger, or exhaustion—decisions people later regret.

The Real Takeaway

A seasoned Texas divorce attorney serves multiple roles:

- Strategist
- Negotiator
- Advocate
- Problem-solver
- Protector

You do not need to be an expert in family law to get through a divorce, but you need someone who is. The right attorney doesn't take over your life; they help you regain control of it.

CHAPTER 23:

Eleven Questions to Ask Yourself and a Divorce Lawyer Before You Hire One

Finding the right divorce attorney is one of the most important decisions you'll make for your case. The stakes are high, the timelines are tight, and the wrong choice can cost you time with your children, financial security, or peace of mind. This is not about finding the flashiest website or the lowest hourly rate. It is about finding the right fit for your situation.

The best way to do that is to ask the right questions. The ones I've outlined in this chapter are designed to help you evaluate potential attorneys clearly, spot red flags early on, and make decisions you won't regret later.

Why These Questions Matter

Hiring a divorce lawyer is not about outsourcing decisions; it is about choosing a guide. You are looking for someone who:

- Listen carefully
- Understands your priorities
- Knows Texas family law
- Can protect your interests without creating unnecessary conflict

The questions below will help you assess all of that.

1. Do You Feel Comfortable with This Lawyer?

Legal skill matters, but so does trust. Ask yourself:

- Do I feel heard and respected?
- Are my questions being answered clearly?
- Can I be honest with this person about difficult details?

If the answer to any of these is no, keep looking. You'll need open communication during your case.

2. Does Attorney Focus on Texas Family Law?

Family law is nuanced and specific. You do not want a generalist, so be sure to ask:

- Is family law their primary practice area?
- How much experience do they have with Texas divorce cases?
- Have they handled situations like mine?

Experience in Texas family law matters far more than any generic credentials.

3. What Is the Attorney's Record Like Overall?

Every divorce is unique, but patterns exist. Ask whether the attorney has handled:

- Custody disputes
- Complex property division

- Business interests or retirement accounts
- Protective orders or CPS involvement

Your confidence in their experience is just as important as their courtroom demonstrative skills.

4. How Does Attorney Approach Conflict?

Divorce requires balance. Ask:

- Do they favor negotiation, litigation, or a strategic mix of both?
- How do they handle situations with intense conflicts?
- How do they keep cases from escalating unnecessarily?

You want someone who is firm but thoughtful, not reckless or passive.

5. How Will Communication Work?

Poor communication is one of the most common complaints in family law cases. Clarify:

- How quickly calls or emails are typically returned
- Whether you'll work directly with the attorney or through their staff
- How updates will be delivered to you

Set expectations early on for the best outcomes.

6. Will You Receive Copies of All Case Documents?

Transparency matters. You should receive copies of:

- Pleadings and motions
- Court orders
- Settlement proposals

If an attorney is vague about or late in sharing documents, that's a red flag.

7. How Are Fees Structured?

Divorce attorneys in Texas typically bill hourly and require a retainer when you begin working together. Some uncontested matters may qualify for flat fees. Ask:

- What is their hourly rate?
- How is the retainer handled?
- How often are invoices sent?
- What happens if the retainer is exhausted?

The goal is not to find the cheapest lawyer, but to understand how the costs align with the value of their work.

8. Are There Any Disciplinary Issues on Their Record?

You can verify an attorney's standing through the State Bar of Texas, but it is also reasonable to ask them directly. An ethical attorney will answer honestly.

9. What Do Online Reviews Say, and What Do They Miss?

Reviews can provide insight into an attorney's communication style and responsiveness, but they do not tell the whole story. Look for patterns, not perfection, and remember that the best legal outcomes aren't always reflected online.

10. How Will You Be Kept Informed About Your Case?

Ask how often you can expect updates and how decisions will be conveyed. Clear communication can prevent frustration and help you stay involved in the process.

11. Do You Trust This Attorney's Judgment?

These may be the most important questions of all.

- Do I trust this person to guide me when my emotions run high?
- Will they tell me the truth, even when it is uncomfortable?
- Do I feel confident putting important decisions in their hands?

If the answer to each of these questions is yes, you are likely making the right choice.

The Real Takeaway

Choosing a divorce lawyer is not about winning an argument or hiring the most aggressive advocate. It is about selecting someone who understands the law, respects your goals, and can guide you through a difficult transition with clarity and integrity. Ask thoughtful questions. Trust your instincts. Choose someone you can work with, not just someone who speaks well.

CHAPTER 24:

Why Are These Questions Important?

Choosing a divorce lawyer is not just a legal decision; it is a strategic one. Divorce is emotionally exhausting, legally complex, and often overwhelming. When people are under this kind of stress, they tend to rush into decisions or rely on convenience instead of clarity. That's how people end up hiring the wrong attorney. It is not that they didn't care; they didn't slow down enough to ask the right questions.

Those listed in the previous chapter exist to protect you from that. They are not about checking boxes; they are about avoiding regret.

These Questions Protect You When Emotions Run High

Divorce clouds judgment. Fear, anger, guilt, and urgency can push people to hire the first attorney who sounds confident or promises fast results—asking thoughtful questions forces you to pause and take the space you need to evaluate not just credentials, but communication style, judgment, and how all of these things align with your goals. That often prevents people from making many of the mistakes I often see occur early on in cases.

Trust and Comfort Are Not "Soft" Factors

Feeling comfortable with your attorney is not a luxury; it is a requirement. You will need to share personal, financial, and sometimes embarrassing details. You will need to hear advice you won't like. If you do not trust your lawyer or feel respected by them, communication breaks down and cases suffer.

Careful questions are about establishing comfort, responsiveness, and communication. They are designed to ensure that the relationship works under pressure, not just at the first meeting.

Experience and Focus Shape Outcomes

Family law is not interchangeable with other areas of practice. It involves nuanced rules, discretionary decisions made by judges, and long-term consequences that general practice experience does not prepare someone for. Questions about specialization, experience with similar cases, and handling complex issues help ensure that the attorney you hire has navigated situations like yours, not just read or heard about them.

Transparency Prevents Future Conflict

Many post-divorce problems stem from misunderstandings that arise early in the attorney-client relationship. Clear discussions about fees, billing practices, document access, and updates can help prevent this frustration. When you set expectations right away, you take a step in preserving trust, even when cases become difficult. Questions about costs, communication, and access to documents are about maintaining control and clarity throughout the process.

Ethical Standards Matter More than Promises

Divorce is stressful enough without having to worry if your attorney will act ethically, meet deadlines, or follow court rules on your behalf. Questions about disciplinary history and reputation aren't about suspicion, but about professionalism. An attorney with strong ethical standards protects not just your case, but your credibility with the court.

Experience Provides Foresight

Attorneys who have handled cases like yours can often anticipate problems before they arise. They recognize patterns, know when disputes tend to escalate, and understand how judges typically respond to general circumstances. That foresight can save you time, money, and emotional energy.

The Real Purpose of These Questions

These questions are not designed to intimidate attorneys, but to empower you. They shift you from passive consumer to informed decision-maker. They help ensure that the attorney you choose is not just qualified, but is right for you.

The Bottom Line

Hiring a divorce lawyer is one of the most important decisions you'll make during this process. Taking the time to ask the right questions doesn't slow you down; it protects you from costly missteps. More importantly, the right attorney will welcome these questions, and the wrong one will avoid them. Knowing the difference can change everything that follows.

CHAPTER 25:

Beware of Common Tricks and Pitfalls

Divorce is difficult even when both spouses act in good faith. When one spouse does not, the process can become far more complicated, not to mention damaging. Over the years, I've seen the same tactics employed again and again. They aren't clever or new, but they are effective when the other side is not prepared to react accordingly.

This chapter is about awareness. Knowing what to watch out for and how to respond can protect your rights, your finances, and your relationships with your children.

Hidden Assets and Financial Games

One of the most common tactics in divorce is hiding or minimizing assets. This can include:

- Undisclosed bank accounts
- Cash sent to friends or family members
- Assets they've intentionally undervalued
- Sudden "losses" or unexplained expenses

The goal is to reduce what appears available for division. Warning signs often include sudden secrecy regarding finances, missing statements, or behavior that doesn't match prior patterns. This is when documentation matters most. In some cases, forensic accountants may be necessary to uncover the full picture. Courts take financial deception seriously, but they can only address what can be proven.

Manipulating Child Custody

Custody manipulation is one of the most damaging—legally and emotionally—tactics I see. This can involve:

- Bad-mouthing the other parent
- Undermining parental authority
- Limiting communication between the child and the other parent
- Using the child as leverage in negotiations

Courts view these behaviors negatively, especially when they harm a child's emotional well-being. If you suspect this is happening, avoid responding emotionally. Maintain consistent communication with your child, document concerning behavior, and consult with your attorney. Judges focus heavily on which parent supports a healthy relationship between the other and the children involved.

Social Media Missteps

Social media has become a common source of evidence in divorce cases. Posts can be used to:

- Misrepresent a person's income or lifestyle
- Undermine custody claims
- Contradict sworn testimony

Even posts used to vent or joke can be taken out of context. The safest approach is caution. Limit your posting, review privacy settings, and assume that anything you share could appear in court. If you are unsure, ask your attorney before posting anything.

Delay Tactics

Some spouses attempt to exhaust the other by dragging out the process. This may include:

- Failing to provide documents promptly
- Ignoring deadlines
- Canceling mediation or depositions
- Repeatedly changing positions in arguments

Delay is often a strategy, not an accident. Staying organized, meeting your own deadlines, and allowing your attorney to apply pressure through the court when necessary can prevent them from working.

Falsifying Financial Information

Beyond hiding assets, some spouses falsify financial documents entirely. This can include:

- Underreporting income
- Fabricating expenses
- Altering other records

Red flags include sudden financial losses, inconsistent statements, or claims that do not align with previously stated facts. If you suspect falsification, immediately bring it to your attorney's attention. Courts have tools to compel disclosure and penalize dishonesty, but again, proof is required.

Emotional Manipulation

Divorce inspires emotional vulnerability, and some spouses exploit that. Tactics can include:

- Guilt-tripping
- Gaslighting
- Threats involving children or finances
- Pressuring the other spouse to make decisions while under stress

Emotional manipulation clouds judgment and often leads to agreements people later regret. Protecting yourself means slowing down, relying on objective advice, and seeking emotional support outside the legal process when needed. An attorney provides a legal perspective; a therapist can help with emotional resilience. Both have a role in this process.

Misuse of Restraining or Protective Orders

Protective orders exist to ensure safety. Unfortunately, they are sometimes misused to gain leverage in custody or property disputes. False or exaggerated allegations can result in immediate restrictions on parenting time and on a spouse's credibility. If this happens, legal response must be swift and precise. Evidence and calm advocacy are both essential. These situations should never be handled without experienced legal guidance.

Settlement Pressure

Settlement pressure is another common tactic. This may involve:

- Artificial deadlines
- Threats of increased costs
- Emotional ultimatums
- Pressure to sign agreements before fully understanding the terms

A rushed settlement is often a bad one. You have the right to review and thoroughly evaluate any agreement before signing it. If something feels wrong, pause. Agreements reached under pressure frequently lead to enforcement or modification battles later.

The Real Takeaway

Most divorce cases do not involve extreme misconduct, but when unethical tactics come into play, awareness is your best defense. Staying informed, documenting everything carefully, and relying on experienced legal guidance can help prevent these strategies from working. Divorce is difficult enough without being constantly caught off guard. Knowing what to expect and how to respond keeps the process fair and protects what matters most.

CHAPTER 26:

How the Texas Divorce Process Unfolds

Understanding the steps of divorce is one thing. Living through them is another.

By this point in the book, you already have a basic understanding of how divorce works in Texas. This chapter is about what people experience at each stage, where mistakes often occur, and why preparation matters more than most people expect. No two divorces are identical, but they all move through the same legal framework.

Filing and First Reactions

Divorce officially begins when a petition has been filed. Emotionally, however, it often begins much earlier with fear, uncertainty, and assumptions about what will happen next. For the filing spouse, the process feels proactive. For the responding spouse, it often feels sudden and disorienting. Responding properly, meeting deadlines, and avoiding emotional reactions can prevent long-term disadvantages.

Temporary Orders and Discovery

Once a case is underway, the focus shifts to **temporary stability**. Temporary orders establish rules for:

- Parenting schedules
- Financial responsibilities
- Use of property

They are not permanent, but they often shape how the rest of the case unfolds.

At the same time, discovery begins. Information is exchanged regarding finances, records, and testimony. Discovery is not about fighting; it is about clarity. When handled correctly, it removes surprises; when ignored, it gives the other side leverage.

Resolution: Settlement or Trial

Most Texas divorces resolve without trial. Negotiation and mediation allow families to control outcomes rather than placing every decision in a judge's hands. These processes are typically faster, less expensive, and emotionally easier—especially when children are involved. Trials are necessary only when agreements cannot be reached via other means. Then, preparation, credibility, and evidence matter far more than theatrics.

When Everything Becomes Real

The divorce decree is not just paperwork; it is a binding court order. It governs:

- Custody and visitation
- Support obligations
- Property division
- Enforcement rights

Vague or poorly drafted decrees can create problems that affect you years later. Clear, enforceable orders protect people long after intense emotions fade.

Life After Divorce

Divorce does not always end a conflict, but it does end uncertainty. That said, even after a divorce is finalized, issues can still arise.

- Missed support payments
- Schedule violations
- Changes in income or other circumstances

Texas law allows enforcement and modification when appropriate. Knowing when and how to act can prevent small problems from becoming major ones.

The Bigger Picture

Divorce is not one decision; it is a series of them. People who understand the process make better choices, protect themselves more effectively, and move forward with fewer regrets.

CHAPTER 27:

The Five Deadly Sins of Divorce

By this point in the book, you have a general understanding of how divorce works in Texas. You know the myths to ignore, the process to expect, and the strategies that can protect your future.

This chapter is about the five mistakes I see most often. They do not happen because people are careless or malicious, but because they are overwhelmed, emotional, or trying to survive a process they never wanted to be part of in the first place. Avoiding these five errors can dramatically improve your outcome, regardless of the complexity of your case.

Sin #1: Hiding or Minimizing Assets

Nothing damages credibility faster than being dishonest about your finances. Some people hide their assets out of fear. Others convince themselves that it is only temporary or that nobody will ever find out. Courts are far less forgiving. Hidden assets can include:

- Undisclosed accounts
- Cash sent to friends or family
- Undervalued property
- Incomplete or misleading financial disclosures

Judges take financial deception seriously. When proven, the consequences of doing this often outweigh whatever someone hoped to gain. Transparency and documentation protect you. Anything else usually backfires.

Sin #2: Letting Emotions Drive Decisions

Divorce is emotional; that's unavoidable. Letting emotions control your decisions is a choice.

Anger, fear, guilt, and grief push people into impulsive choices that can lead to unnecessary conflict, unreasonable demands, or agreements made to end the pain. Clients typically regret those decisions later, but feeling emotional is normal. Acting on it without a strategy is what may cost you. Slow down, seek objective advice, and separate emotion from your decision-making process as much as possible.

Sin #3: Ignoring the Advice of Your Attorney

Hiring an attorney and then disregarding their guidance is one of the most self-defeating choices people can make. Your attorney understands the law and the likely consequences of each move. Ignoring their expertise out of frustration, pride, or exhaustion often leads to avoidable setbacks. If you disagree with their advice, ask questions. Do not substitute instinct for experience in a process that results in permanent consequences.

Sin #4: Using Children as Leverage

Using children—directly or indirectly—is one of the most damaging mistakes in divorce. This can include:

- Bad-mouthing the other parent
- Limiting access
- Involving children in disputes between adults
- Using parenting time as an opportunity to negotiate or pressure

Courts take this behavior seriously. More importantly, children feel it deeply. Judges consistently favor parents who support a healthy relationship between the children and their other parent, even when the marriage is ending. Protecting your children also protects your case.

Sin #5: Failing to Plan for Life After Divorce

Divorce doesn't end with a final decree; it begins a new chapter. People who focus only on getting through a divorce often fail to plan for what comes next. That lack of planning creates instability long after the case is closed. Planning means:

- Understanding post-divorce finances
- Anticipating housing and budgeting changes
- Preparing for co-parenting realities
- Thinking beyond the immediate conflict

Divorce is not just about resolving the past; it is about positioning yourself for the future.

How to Avoid These Five Mistakes

The people who navigate divorce most successfully tend to do a few things consistently.

- They are honest about finances.
- They slow down when making emotional decisions.
- They trust experienced guidance from their attorney.
- They protect their children from conflict.
- They plan for life beyond the courtroom.

These steps do not require perfection, but awareness.

The Real Takeaway

Divorce is difficult, and mistakes are understandable, but some errors cause lasting damage: legally, financially, and emotionally. Avoiding these sins doesn't guarantee an easy divorce. It does dramatically reduce regret, and that matters.

CHAPTER 28:

You Are Not Broken, but Transitioning

If you have made it this far, there's something important I want you to hear. You are not weak, failing, or behind in any way. You are in transition.

Most people do not approach divorce confidently. They feel disoriented, scared, angry, exhausted—sometimes all at once. That doesn't mean something is wrong. It just means you are facing a major life change without a roadmap, and most people do not realize how disorienting that is until they are in it.

I've watched thousands of people walk through divorce. Those who struggle the most aren't unintelligent, unmotivated, or careless. They are overwhelmed. They are trying to make decisions while being emotionally flooded. They are guessing instead of grounding themselves in facts, and guessing is where people can get hurt.

Divorce Is Not a Moral Judgment

One of the most damaging ideas people perpetuate is that getting a divorce says something about their worth. It doesn't.

Divorce is a structured legal process, and a predictable one once you understand how it works. The court is not there to decide who is the better person. It exists to resolve specific legal questions regarding custody, property, support, and future rights. When people stop viewing divorce as a personal indictment and start seeing it as a process to navigate, everything changes. Fear melts away, decision-making improves, and outcomes stabilize. That shift alone can save people years of regret.

Fear Is Normal, but Letting It Drive You Is Optional

Fear makes people rush, overshare, hide things they shouldn't, and listen to the wrong voices, like those of their friends, relatives, social media personalities, or someone else's bad experience dressed up as advice. I've seen people lose time with their children because they panicked, and money because they were exhausted and just wanted it all to be over. I've also seen people damage their credibility by reacting instead of thinking. None of that was inevitable.

The people who come out on the other side of a divorce with a positive outcome aren't the loudest or the most aggressive. They slowed down enough to make clear decisions, understood what mattered and ignored what didn't, and didn't try to win everything. Instead, they protected what counted most.

You Do Not Need to Control Everything.

One of the most comforting truths I can offer is that you do not need to understand every detail of the law. You do not need to predict every outcome or fight every battle. You need clarity, honest advice, and a strategy grounded in reality. When people accept that, their stress levels drop dramatically. They stop reacting to every message or rumor. They stop chasing emotional wins that ultimately cost them. They start thinking about their children, their finances, and their ability to move forward in the long run. That's when divorce stops feeling like chaos and starts feeling manageable.

What I've Learned After Hundreds of Cases

After years of practicing family law, I've noticed that the people who come out of a divorce strongest aren't the ones who think they won the most arguments. They are the ones who protected their credibility, followed court orders, documented rather than escalated, and stayed focused on outcomes rather than revenge. They didn't try to use the system as a weapon; they used it as a tool, and it worked far better than they expected in the end.

An Invitation, not a Sales Pitch

If you need help, ask for it early on. Guessing is expensive.

If you work with my firm, we'll take this process seriously and treat you with respect. If you do not, find someone who understands Texas family law and who will tell you the truth even when it is uncomfortable. What matters most is that you do not navigate this alone or unthinkingly. You do not have to rush, panic, or get everything right immediately. You have to stop guessing.

A Final Thought

Divorce feels like an ending, but it is usually just another one of life's turning points. How it works out depends less on what happened during your marriage and more on how you handle what comes next.

If this book helped you feel calmer, more informed, or more grounded, then it did exactly what I hoped it would do. You are not broken or failing. You are transitioning, and with the right information and support, you can come through this stronger and ready for what is next.

CHAPTER 29:

Do not Face This Journey Alone!

By the time you reach this chapter, you already know more than most people do at the start of a divorce. You understand how the process works, which myths to ignore, and how easily fear and bad advice can derail good intentions. That puts you ahead.

What happens next is a choice. You can move forward on your own using what you have learned; if you do, this book has served its purpose. Alternatively, you may determine that a matter of this significance warrants the expertise and strategic guidance of an experienced advisor.

After years of handling divorce cases in Texas, I can tell you that the people who get the best outcomes do not wait until things spiral out of control to ask for help. They get clarity early on, protect their credibility, and avoid expensive mistakes—or sometimes impossible-to-fix ones—to fix later.

If you choose to work with my firm, you'll get straight answers, a clear plan, and guidance grounded in Texas law, not fear, pressure, or false promises. We focus on outcomes that make sense long after the divorce is final. Divorce is navigable, but only if you move forward deliberately. If you want to talk through your situation and understand your options, call my office. A simple conversation now can prevent years of regret later.

Take action today toward

Your new future!

Call our office today and
Make your appointment for a
free consultation (a $500 value).

281-810-9760

ABOUT THE AUTHOR

Bryan Fagan is a Texas family law attorney, husband, and father of three who has spent his career helping families navigate divorce, custody disputes, and other complex matters with clarity, strategy, and purpose.

Born in Denver and raised in Atascocita, Texas, Bryan developed an early interest in the law and a strong commitment to service. While attending South Texas College of Law, he cared for his grandmother during the day. He attended classes at night—an experience that shaped his practical, client-centered approach to legal problem-solving.

In 2012, Bryan founded the Law Office of Bryan Fagan, PLLC. What began as a small practice has grown into one of the largest family law firms in Texas, with more than 170 team members focused exclusively on family law, including divorce, child custody and support, CPS defense, adoption, and related matters.

Bryan is a member of the College of the State Bar of Texas and is widely recognized for his emphasis on client education, clear communication, and disciplined legal strategy. His approach is grounded in the belief that informed clients make better decisions and that clarity reduces conflict, cost, and regret.

Bryan also values time with his wife and children, remains active in his church, and mentors young professionals entering the legal field.

Made in the USA
Monee, IL
04 November 2026

67380056R00066